Tab

by Ethan Cruz
illustrated by Paige Keiser

Core Decodable 62

Mc Graw Hill Education

Bothell, WA • Chicago, IL • Columbus, OH • New York, NY

MHEonline.com

McGraw-Hill Education

Copyright © 2015 McGraw-Hill Education

All rights reserved. No part of this publication may be reproduced or distributed in any form or by any means, or stored in a database or retrieval system, without the prior written consent of McGraw-Hill Education, including, but not limited to, network storage or transmission, or broadcast for distance learning.

Send all inquiries to:
McGraw-Hill Education
8787 Orion Place
Columbus, OH 43240

ISBN: 978-0-02-143446-6
MHID: 0-02-143446-8

Printed in the United States of America.

2 3 4 5 6 7 8 9 DOC 20 19 18 17 16 15

Did the back gate shut?
Jane looked at the handle.

The gate did not shut.
Jane's kitten, Tab, left the yard.

Did Tab run fast?
Yes, quick Tab ran down Apple Lane.

Jane had to chase her kitten.
"Stop, Tab!" she yelled.

Kate set down her bottles.
"I will help," she said.

Tab ran past men with rakes.
The men helped and yelled, "Stop, Tab!"

Jason had seven bundles of paper.
"I can help!" he yelled.

Little Tab ran and ran.
This game of chase was fun.

Val was in her van.
"I will help," she yelled.

"Stop, Tab!"

Kate and Jason yelled and helped.

Val and the men yelled and helped.

Tab made a quick turn.
Jane did not see her.

"This is a puzzle," said Jane.
"I cannot see Tab."

Barb spotted the chase a little later.
She chuckled and checked on Tab.

"Tab is back," said Barb.
"Tab is safe under the table."